Date: 10/17/11

Pennie Stoyles

The A-Z of
Health

Volume 1 A–B

Smart Apple Media
P.O. Box 3263
Mankato, MN, 56002

First published in 2010 by
MACMILLAN EDUCATION AUSTRALIA PTY LTD
15–19 Claremont St, South Yarra, Australia 3141

Visit our web site at www.macmillan.com.au or go directly to www.macmillanlibrary.com.au

Associated companies and representatives throughout the world.

Copyright © Pennie Stoyles 2010

Library of Congress Cataloging-in-Publication Data

Stoyles, Pennie.
   The A-Z of health / Pennie Stoyles.
       p. cm.
   Includes index.
   ISBN 978-1-59920-541-0 (library binding)
   ISBN 978-1-59920-542-7 (library binding)
   ISBN 978-1-59920-543-4 (library binding)
   ISBN 978-1-59920-544-1 (library binding)
   ISBN 978-1-59920-545-8 (library binding)
   ISBN 978-1-59920-546-5 (library binding)
   1. Medicine, Popular—Encyclopedias, Juvenile. 2. Health—Encyclopedias, Juvenile. I. Title.
   RC81.A2S76 2011
616.003--dc22

2009038467

Edited by Julia Carlomagno and Gill Owens
Text and cover design by Ivan Finnegan, iF Design
Page layout by Raul Diche
Photo research by Legend Images
Illustrations by Andy Craig and Nives Porcellato

Manufactured in China by Macmillan Production (Asia) Ltd.
Kwun Tong, Kowloon, Hong Kong
Supplier Code: CP December 2009

Acknowledgments
The author and the publisher are grateful to the following for permission to reproduce copyright material:

Front cover photo of a boy using an asthma inhaler © Peter Elvidge/iStockphoto

Photographs courtesy of:
© Stephanie Maze/Corbis, **11** (top); © Dr. Milton Reisch/Corbis, **5**; © Bernard Bisson/Sygma/Corbis, **20**; Andy Crawford © Dorling Kindersley, **31**; Image Source, **25**; © 2008 Jupiterimages Corporation, **9**, **14**, **17** (bottom), **22**; National Archives Australia, A1200, L1592, 15 (bottom); National Library of Medicine, Images from the History of Medicine (IHM), **11** (bottom); © Newspix/News Ltd/Toby Zerna, **18**; PHIL/CDC/C. Goldsmith, **6**; PHIL/CDC/Janice Haney Carr, **23**; PHIL/CDC/Emory Univ.; Dr. Sellers, **8**; Photodisc, **19**; Photolibrary/Medicimage, **12**; Photolibrary/Martyn Chillmaid/OSF, **16**; Photolibrary/CNRI/SPL, **15** (top); Photolibrary/MICHAEL DONNE/SPL, **13**; © Ann Baldwin/Shutterstock, **27**; © sonya etchison/Shutterstock, **29**; © Jerome Tabet, **21**; © Veer Incorporated, **17** (top).
Map based on data from World Health Organisation/UNAIDS, 2008, **7**.

Health

Welcome to the exciting world of health.

The A–Z of Health is about the healthy functioning of the body and mind.
Health can mean:

- physical and mental health, including different body processes
- diseases and illnesses that affect health and well-being
- drugs, treatments, and ways to stay healthy

Volume 1 A–B   Health

They Said It!

"Health is a state of complete physical, mental and social well being, not merely the absence of disease."

World Health Organization (WHO) Constitution, 1948

Acne

Acne is the name for different types of pimples that form when pores, or tiny holes in the skin, become blocked and **infected**.

How Acne Forms

Each pore contains a hair gland and an oil gland. The oil made in the oil gland keeps the skin soft and helps remove dead skin cells. Sometimes an oil gland produces too much oil and blocks the pore. **Bacteria** then collect in the blocked pore. If the blockage is black, it is called a blackhead. If the blockage is white, it is called a whitehead. If the blockage becomes infected, it fills with pus and it is called a pustule.

What Causes Acne?

Acne can be caused when a person's body produces too much oil. Many teenagers get acne during adolescence, a period in which their bodies are changing. Acne can also be caused by using oily skin creams or makeup, which can clog pores. Some people get more acne in hot weather, because they sweat a lot. Acne can also run in families.

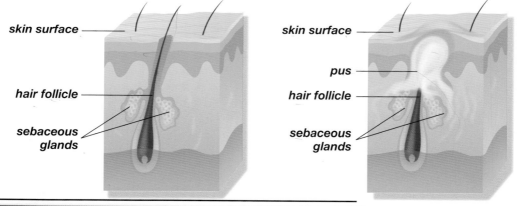

skin surface

hair follicle

sebaceous glands

skin surface

pus

hair follicle

sebaceous glands

While an unblocked pore (left) contains a normal amount of oil, a blocked pore (right) contains an excessive amount of oil and pus, which causes a bump on the skin's surface.

Did You Know?

There are many myths about what causes acne. Some people believe that eating chocolate causes pimples, but scientific tests have not proven this.

Treating and Preventing Acne

Acne can be treated with lotions or creams that contain ingredients to dry up oil and kill bacteria. Doctors can also **prescribe** drugs to treat severe acne.

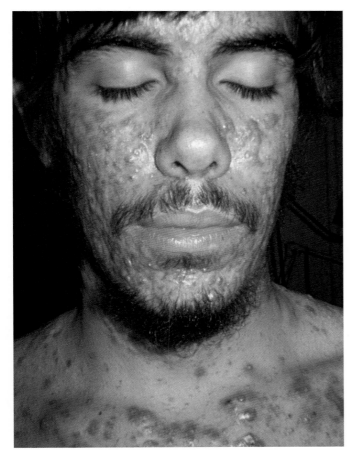

This man has severe acne on his forehead, cheeks, and chest.

The best way to prevent acne is to wash skin regularly with a gentle soap. People suffering from acne should try not to touch their skin. They should not pick or squeeze pimples, as this could spread the infection and cause more pimples. Acne sufferers should also avoid using oily creams and makeup.

Did You Know?

Acne can affect people of any age, from babies to adults. However, teenagers are at the highest risk of developing acne. About three in every four teenagers develop some form of acne.

GLOSSARY WORDS

infected	filled with disease-producing germs
bacteria	microscopic, single-celled living things
prescribe	recommend a drug to be taken to treat a particular illness

Acquired Immune Deficiency Syndrome

Acquired Immune Deficiency Syndrome (AIDS) is a disease in which the **immune system** breaks down. People with AIDS can have difficulty fighting even minor infections.

AIDS and HIV

AIDS is caused by a **virus** called Human Immunodeficiency Virus (HIV). HIV "reprograms" a person's CD4 cells, which are cells that help fight infection. When people with HIV contract an illness, the CD4 cells do not fight the infection but instead produce more HIV. At the same time, the CD4 cells are destroyed. People with HIV may show no signs of illness, and may live a healthy life. If they become ill, they are said to have AIDS.

How HIV Is Spread

People can get HIV if they come in contact with bodily fluids, such as blood, from an infected person. Some people get HIV during **sexual intercourse**. Mothers who have HIV can sometimes pass it on to their babies during pregnancy or birth.

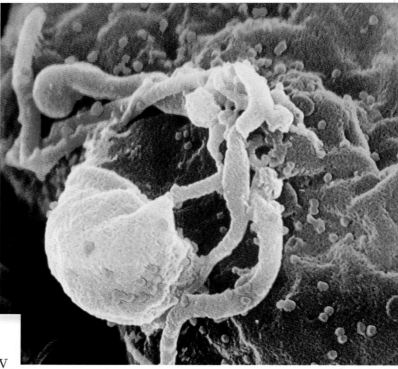

Under a microscope, scientists can see the HIV virus (shown in pink) attaching itself to a healthy cell (shown in blue).

? Did You Know?

It is not possible to become infected with HIV by sharing food, shaking hands, or touching the same objects as an infected person.

Preventing AIDS and HIV

There are no cures for AIDS and HIV, so it is very important to prevent the spread of HIV. Hospitals clean their surgical equipment very carefully so that there is no chance of infecting someone accidentally. Blood used in **blood transfusions** is tested to make sure that it is not infected with HIV, and injections are given with disposable needles. People can also use protection during sexual intercourse.

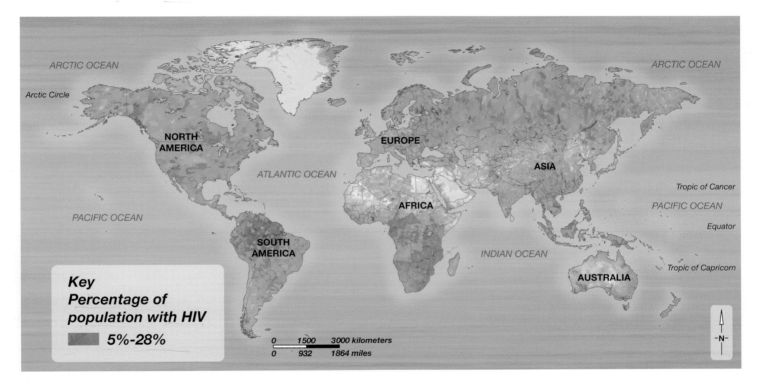

Key
Percentage of population with HIV
5%-28%

The orange areas on this map show where HIV is most common. Many African countries have been seriously affected by AIDS and HIV.

Did You Know?

World AIDS Day is held on December 1 every year. In the lead-up to this day, people raise money by selling red ribbons. The money is used to look after people with AIDS and to fund research into a cure. The first World AIDS Day was held in 1988.

GLOSSARY WORDS

immune system	a network of systems in the body that fights germs and diseases
virus	microscopic living particles that stop cells from working properly
sexual intercourse	sexual contact that involves exchanging some bodily fluids
blood transfusions	injections of blood from one person into the body of another

Allergies

Allergies occur when people's bodies overreact to something. It could be something they touch, eat, or breathe in, or something that is injected into them.

How Allergies Occur

Blood contains white blood cells, which destroy harmful **bacteria**, **viruses**, and poisons that enter the body. People with allergies have white blood cells that cannot tell the difference between harmful substances and substances that are usually harmless. As the white blood cells try to fight off the substance, they release **histamines** (say hist-UH-meens), which cause an allergic reaction.

Allergens

An allergen is anything that causes an allergy. Different people can react differently to the same allergen. Allergens can cause itchiness, watery eyes, runny noses, sneezing, breathing difficulties, skin rashes, vomiting, and **diarrhea**.

Common allergens include:

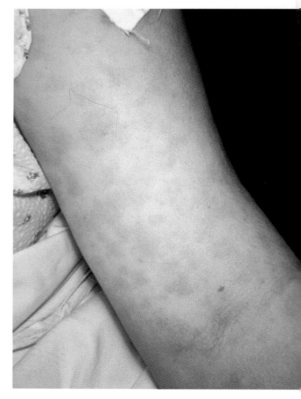

- pollens and dust, which can cause hay fever
- insect bites, such as those from bees and wasps
- soaps and lotions
- foods, such as peanuts and shellfish
- drugs, such as penicillin

 FIRST AID

Epinephrine Autoinjectors

Anaphylaxis can be treated with an injection of a drug called epinephrine. People with severe allergies often carry epinephrine autoinjectors, such as EpiPens, which are needles that automatically inject the correct dose of epinephrine. In some countries, all teachers must be trained to use epinephrine autoinjectors in case a student experiences anaphylaxis.

This rash was caused by an allergic reaction to penicillin.

Anaphylaxis

People who are very sensitive to a particular allergen can have a severe allergic reaction called anaphylaxis (say ana-FUH-lak-SUHS). People with anaphylaxis can become itchy and swollen all over. They may have breathing difficulties, and their blood pressure will drop. If they do not receive urgent medical attention, they may go into **anaphylactic shock**. Many people die of anaphylactic shock each year.

This girl is using an asthma inhaler to treat her asthma.

Did You Know?

Asthma is a lung disease that may be caused by an allergy. People who suffer from asthma often use an asthma inhaler to help them breathe.

GLOSSARY WORDS

bacteria	microscopic, single-celled living things
viruses	microscopic living particles that stop cells from working properly
histamines	chemicals released into the bloodstream by white blood cells that help the body fight off bacteria
diarrhea	a disorder in the intestines that causes runny feces
anaphylactic shock	a severe allergic reaction in which the body may shut down and starve the organs of oxygen

Alzheimer's Disease

Alzheimer's (say alts-HY-muhz) disease is a brain disease that affects the normal function of a person's brain. Alzheimer's disease begins slowly and becomes worse over time.

Alzheimer's Disease and Dementia

Alzheimer's disease is a severe form of **dementia**. Many people suffer from dementia as they get older. Alzheimer's disease often starts earlier in life and becomes worse at a faster rate as people get older. People with Alzheimer's disease first forget little things, such as where they left the car keys, but can eventually forget major things, such as how to get dressed, how to drive, and even who their relatives are. Eventually, people with Alzheimer's disease become so ill that they cannot speak or feed themselves.

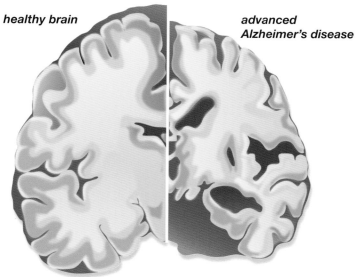

healthy brain

advanced Alzheimer's disease

The brain of a person suffering from Alzheimer's disease (right) is much smaller than a normal brain (left).

Causes of Alzheimer's Disease

The human brain is composed of billions of nerve cells, which send messages to one another. As people get older, some of the nerve cells die and messages cannot be sent as easily. People with Alzheimer's disease have damaged nerve cells and **plaques**. This means that parts of their brains that normally work together are disconnected.

HEALTH PROFESSIONALS: Geriatricians

Geriatricians are doctors who are specially trained to look after elderly people. They prevent and treat diseases that affect people as they get older, such as Alzheimer's disease.

Cures for Alzheimer's Disease

Currently, there is no effective treatment or cure for Alzheimer's disease. Scientists and doctors are researching the causes of the disease and looking for ways to prevent or cure it. A **vaccine** has been developed but has not yet been tested successfully.

People with Alzheimer's disease may need help with basic tasks, such as combing their hair.

Alois Alzheimer (1865–1915)

Alois Alzheimer was a German psychiatrist who first described the signs of a disease he called "presenile dementia" in 1906. Another psychiatrist, Emil Kraepelin, renamed it Alzheimer's disease in honor of Alzheimer.

GLOSSARY WORDS

dementia   loss of some mental powers
plaques   clumps of dead nerve cells
vaccine   a small dose of a virus or bacteria injected into patients to help their bodies fight off disease

Anesthetics

Anesthetics (say an-ES-thet-ICKS) are drugs that make patients numb or unconscious, so that they do not feel pain during operations. The word "anesthetic" means "without sensation."

Benefits of Anesthetics

There are many benefits to using anesthetics. Without anesthetics, **surgeons** and dentists would not be able to perform major operations without the patient feeling any pain. Some women have anesthetics to ease the pain of childbirth.

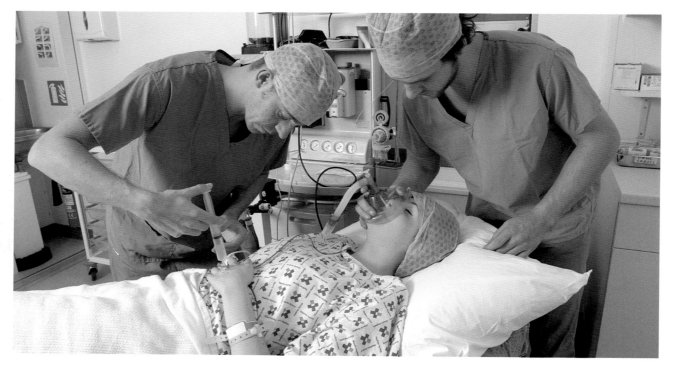

An anesthesiologist gives patients a general anesthetic before they undergo a major operation.

HEALTH PROFESSIONALS: Anesthesiologists

Anesthesiologists are trained doctors who administer anesthetics during operations. They carefully measure the amount of anesthetic a patient needs according to his or her weight and health. They also check a patient's breathing, heartbeat, and blood pressure.

Types of Anesthetics

There are many different types of anesthetics.

- Local anesthetics are usually given by injection into a particular nerve. They numb only a small area of the body, so patients stay awake and alert.

- General anesthetics are given either by injection or by **inhalation**. They make patients unconscious and numb all over. Some general anesthetics put patients into such a deep sleep that they cannot breathe. The anesthesiologist uses a machine called a ventilator to keep them breathing.

- Epidural anesthetics are given by injection into the spine. They numb the bottom half of the body, but patients stay awake.

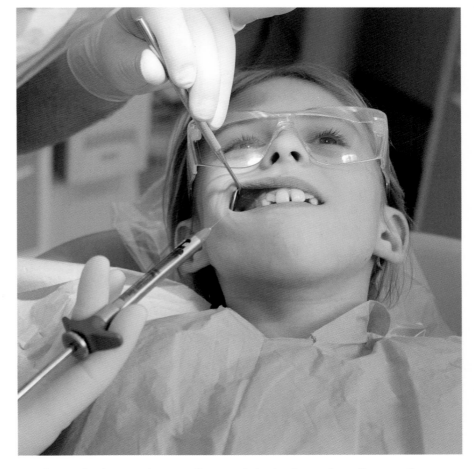

Local anesthetics numb a small area of the body, such as the mouth, while the patient stays awake.

Did You Know?

In China, some medical practitioners use **acupuncture** to anesthetize their patients before operations.

GLOSSARY WORDS

surgeons	doctors trained to perform operations
inhalation	breathing in
acupuncture	a traditional Chinese method of healing, which uses fine needles that are inserted into the skin

Antibiotics

Antibiotics (say an-TIE-buy-OT-iks) are substances that can kill microscopic **organisms** called **bacteria**. The most famous antibiotic, penicillin, is made from a type of mold called *Penicillium*.

Drugs That Save Lives

Antibiotics can save people's lives. Before antibiotics were developed, a patient with an infected wound may have had a body part **amputated** in order to prevent the infection from spreading. Today, an infected wound can be cured in a short period of time by using antibiotics. Once, millions of people died from common illnesses such as pneumonia, but today these illnesses can be treated using antibiotics.

Uses of Antibiotics

Many different antibiotics exist today, and each is used to kill different types of bacteria. Doctors may prescribe antibiotics to treat patients with infections, or to prevent infections from developing in patients with serious cuts or after an operation. Antibiotics are most commonly given as tablets, but may also be given as an injection or as a skin cream or powder.

Antibiotics can be taken as tablets.

Did You Know?

In the 1800s, French scientist Louis Pasteur showed that garlic could be used to kill bacteria. Modern scientific studies have also shown that garlic can be used as an antibiotic, although it is 100 times less effective than penicillin.

Antibiotic Resistance

Over time, bacteria can sometimes develop a resistance to an antibiotic, which means that the antibiotic no longer kills the bacteria. New antibiotics must then be developed to kill the bacteria. Golden staph, a type of bacteria that can cause a range of infections, is now resistant to all known antibiotics. Scientists are working to develop a new antibiotic that will kill it.

Antibiotics can break down and destroy infected cells (shown in orange in this image taken under a microscope).

Alexander Fleming (1881–1955) and Howard Florey (1898–1968)

In 1928, British scientist Alexander Fleming was growing samples of bacteria when one of the samples accidentally became moldy. He noticed that the mold, which was *Penicillium*, was killing the bacteria. Around 1938, a team of scientists, including Australian Howard Florey (shown left), found the active ingredient in *Penicillium* and proved that it could cure serious **bacterial infections**. In 1945, Fleming, Florey, and another scientist, Ernst Chain, shared the Nobel Prize in Medicine for the discovery of penicillin.

GLOSSARY WORDS

organisms	living things
bacteria	microscopic, single-celled living things
amputated	cut off by a surgeon
bacterial infections	illnesses caused by the growth of damaging bacteria

Antiseptics

Antiseptics (say anti-SEP-tiks) are substances that kill **bacteria** and **viruses** or stop them from growing. They are usually used on the skin.

Common Antiseptics

One commonly used antiseptic is iodine. Iodine is a brown liquid that is used to clean cuts and scrapes. It is also used by surgeons to clean a patient before and after an operation.

Another commonly used antiseptic is pure alcohol. Doctors swab a patient's skin with alcohol before they give an injection. Mouthwash, which often contains a high amount of alcohol, is an antiseptic used to kill bacteria that cause tooth decay.

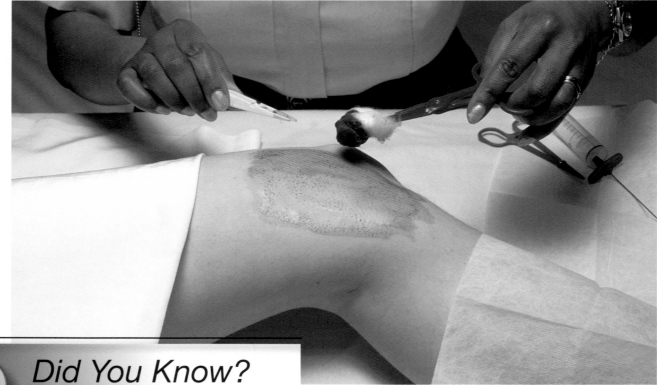

Did You Know?
The word "antiseptic" means "against infection."

Iodine is an antiseptic used to kill bacteria in minor cuts and grazes.

Antiseptics and Surgery

Antiseptics are an important part of any **surgery**. Before antiseptics were discovered, bacteria would often get into a wound during an operation. Many patients developed infections after operations, and some even died. Today, surgeons use antiseptics to clean a patient's skin before an operation. Surgeons and nurses helping with the operation also use antiseptics to wash their hands and arms before putting on surgical gloves. **Disinfectants** are like antiseptics, but they are used on surgical instruments, such as scissors and scalpels, and on other surfaces rather than on skin. Antiseptics are used again after the wound is stitched up and to keep the skin clean as the wound heals.

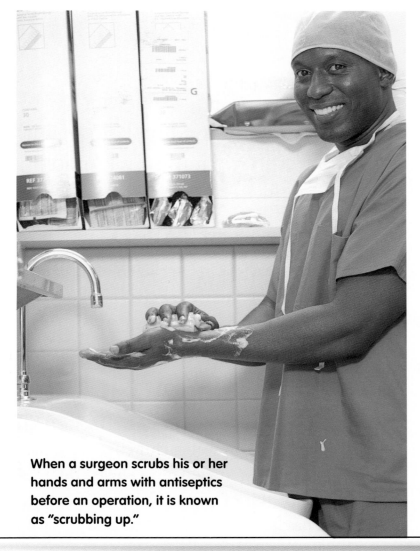

When a surgeon scrubs his or her hands and arms with antiseptics before an operation, it is known as "scrubbing up."

Joseph Lister (1827–1912)

British doctor Joseph Lister was the first person to use antiseptics during surgery. He used a substance called phenol, or carbolic acid, to disinfect surgical instruments and clean patients before operations. He also had it sprayed into the air during operations. In 1879, Listerine® mouthwash was invented and named after Lister for his work in antiseptics.

GLOSSARY WORDS

bacteria	microscopic, single-celled living things
viruses	microscopic living particles that stop cells from working properly
surgery	an operation or treatment performed by a surgeon
disinfectants	chemical substances that kill bacteria on surgical instruments and other surfaces

Attention Deficit Hyperactivity Disorder

Attention Deficit Hyperactivity Disorder (ADHD) is a **behavioral disorder**. People with ADHD have excessive energy and difficulty in concentrating.

Causes of ADHD

There are no known causes of ADHD, although it is thought that the disorder may run in families. Scientists know that approximately 1 in 20 children suffer from ADHD. They have also observed that the brains of children with the disorder seem to work differently from those without it.

Diagnosing ADHD

To decide if a child has ADHD, doctors look at the way the child is behaving. They test how well a child listens to instructions, his or her concentration, and how organized he or she is. Doctors also look for **symptoms** of hyperactive behavior, such as fidgeting and climbing on furniture.

To be **diagnosed** with ADHD, a child must show many different ADHD behaviors over a period of at least six months.

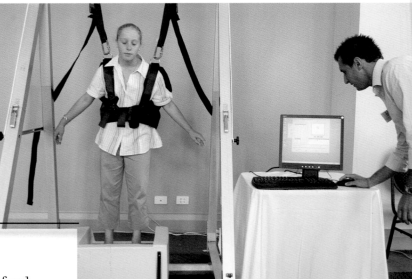

Did You Know?

Scientists have found that some artificial food colorings make some young children hyperactive. If these children stop eating artificially colored foods, their behavior returns to normal.

This girl is demonstrating a balance machine as part of the world's first drug-free treatment to cure ADHD by using exercise programs.

Effects of ADHD

Children with ADHD often suffer from problems at school. They can find it hard to make friends and learn in class. Teachers can help students with ADHD by giving them extra attention when needed. Parents can help by ensuring that their children eat a balanced diet and get plenty of sleep. Doctors can also prescribe drugs for some forms of ADHD.

Some children with ADHD have teacher's aides to help them stay focused in class.

Did You Know?

The terms "hypo" and "hyper" are used at the beginning of many medical words. "Hypo" means "under" and "hyper" means "over." Therefore, "hyperactive" means "overactive," or having too much energy.

GLOSSARY WORDS

behavioral disorder	an illness that affects how people behave
symptoms	signs that a person may be suffering from a particular disease or illness
diagnosed	decided whether someone has a disease by examining them

Autism

Autism is a **complex disorder** in which a person's brain does not develop properly. People with autism have difficulty in communicating and reacting to other people in social situations.

Symptoms of Autism

Symptoms of autism are usually noticed in the first three years of a person's life. Different people will have different combinations of symptoms. Symptoms to do with communication include repeating words and sayings, using nonsense words, or even not speaking at all. Symptoms to do with social situations include having difficulty in making friends, preferring to be alone, and avoiding eye contact and crowds. Some people with autism also have very sensitive skin and do not like loud noises.

Causes of Autism

There are no known causes of autism. It is known that the brains of people with autism function abnormally, but doctors and scientists have not been able to find out what causes this.

This girl is being tested for autism by her doctor, Professor Gilbert Lelord, in Tours, France.

Did You Know?
Autism affects almost four times as many boys as girls.

Savants

Some people with autism are also savants. Savants have extremely good memories for one subject. For example, a savant who is gifted with numbers may be able to memorize all the numbers in the telephone book or calculate difficult mathematical equations. A savant gifted in music may be able to perform a piece of music after hearing it once.

Asperger's Syndrome

Asperger's (say asp-ERG-uhz) Syndrome is a form of autism. People with Asperger's Syndrome have difficulty in understanding non-verbal communication. This means that they may not understand others' facial expressions and gestures or may not use these to communicate. Many people with Asperger's Syndrome like routine and have difficulty in making friends.

Daniel Tammet is a savant famous for his extremely good memory of numbers and languages.

Hans Asperger (1906–1980)

Austrian doctor Hans Asperger worked with children who showed unusual behaviors. In 1944, he described the symptoms of Asperger's Syndrome, which was later named in his honor.

GLOSSARY WORDS

complex disorder	a disorder that is likely caused by a combination of different factors
symptoms	signs that a person may be suffering from a particular disease or illness

Bacteria

Bacteria are microscopic, single-celled living things.
They are found almost everywhere on Earth.

Healthy Bacteria

People come into contact with millions of bacteria every day, many of which keep them healthy. Bacteria are in the air people breathe, in the food they eat, and on most things they touch. Human intestines contain more than 300 types of healthy bacteria. These bacteria help digest food and absorb **nutrients**. Bacteria in the intestines also produce vitamin K, which helps blood to **clot**.

Bacteria in the Environment

Bacteria play an important role in the natural environment. When plants and animals die, bacteria cause their bodies to decay so that nutrients are returned to the soil. Bacteria also cause food scraps and trash to decay. They can also help in the treatment of **sewage**.

Yogurt contains healthy bacteria that are good for the intestines.

Did You Know?

Bacteria are used to make some foods, including yogurt and soy sauce.

Bacteria and Disease

Some bacteria are harmful to the body and cause disease. When harmful bacteria get into the body, they are usually attacked and killed by white blood cells. If the bacteria are not killed, they multiply, spreading through the body and causing disease. Tetanus, cholera, pneumonia, food poisoning, and tooth decay are all **bacterial diseases**.

Bacteria in Food

Harmful bacteria can get into food and cause food poisoning. Covering food will stop bacteria in the air from falling into it. Cooking food usually kills bacteria, and freezing food usually stops bacteria from multiplying. However, some bacteria will stay alive and start to multiply once the food defrosts.

The *Bacillus anthracis* bacteria (magnified here) cause a harmful disease called anthrax.

FIRST AID +

Preventing Infections

People can lower the risk of getting a bacterial infection or disease by:

+ washing their hands after going to the toilet and before eating
+ cleaning their teeth regularly
+ cleaning cuts and scrapes with antiseptic

GLOSSARY WORDS

nutrients	food or chemicals that the body needs to survive
clot	dry and form scabs
sewage	used water and waste from bathrooms and kitchens
bacterial diseases	diseases caused by harmful bacteria that have entered the body

Blood

Blood carries oxygen, **hormones**, nutrients, and wastes around the body and fights infections.

What is Blood?

Blood contains red blood cells, white blood cells, and microscopic disks called platelets, all floating in liquid called plasma.

- Red blood cells carry oxygen from the lungs to every cell in the body.
- White blood cells fight infections.
- Platelets help blood to clot and form scabs when the skin is injured.
- Plasma contains dissolved nutrients, waste, hormones, and **antibodies**.

Iron and Blood

The body needs iron to make red blood cells. People with low levels of iron in their blood cannot make enough red blood cells to carry oxygen around their bodies. These people may develop a disease called anemia (say uh-NEEM-ee-UH). They look pale and feel tired because their cells are not getting enough oxygen.

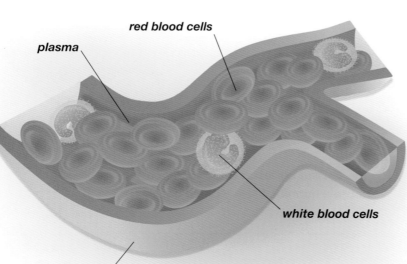

plasma

red blood cells

white blood cells

blood vessel

Blood contains many more red blood cells than white blood cells.

FIRST AID

Controlling Bleeding

In order to control bleeding, press hard on the part of the skin that is bleeding, or bandage it tightly. If possible, raise the bleeding body part above the heart. If a person is bleeding heavily, an ambulance should be called.

Blood Tests

Sometimes a doctor will take a small sample of blood in order to test it. There are many substances in blood that can reveal something about a person's health. For example, the level of sugar in a person's blood can show if his or her liver and pancreas are working properly. An increased number of white blood cells in the blood may mean that a person has an infection.

Blood Pressure

Doctors test blood pressure using a machine called a sphygmomanometer (say sfig-moh-mah-nom-etah). The doctor wraps a band around the patient's arm and pumps it up in order to stop the flow of blood. The doctor then lets the air out slowly to get two readings, the pressure of blood during a heartbeat and the pressure between heartbeats. If a person's blood pressure is high, it means that his or her heart has to pump harder to move blood around the body. People with high blood pressure are at greater risk of having a heart attack.

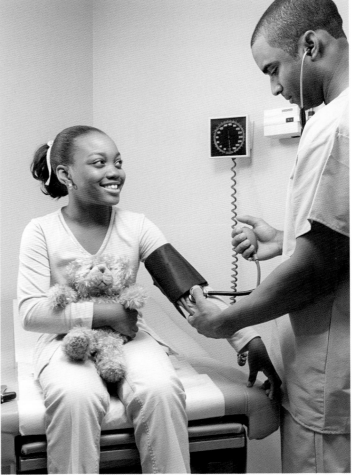

Doctors can check for high blood pressure using a sphygmomanometer.

HEALTH PROFESSIONALS: Hematologists

Hematologists are scientists who study how blood is formed and blood diseases.

GLOSSARY WORDS

hormones chemicals that control how the body works
antibodies chemicals that fight diseases

Bones

Bones make up a skeleton. They protect important organs and help people to move.

Layers of a Bone

Bones may look as if they are dead, but in fact they contain living cells that are growing all the time. The outer surface of a bone contains nerves and **blood vessels**. Beneath this, there is a layer of smooth, hard bone. Then there is a layer of softer bone that looks like a sponge. The center is filled with **marrow**. This is where red blood cells are made.

Keeping Bones Healthy

It is important to keep bones healthy so that they stay strong. Bone cells absorb calcium and turn it into a substance called hydroxyapatite (say hi-drok-see-AP-uh-tite), which is what keeps bones strong. To strengthen bones, people can exercise and eat dairy foods that are high in calcium, such as milk, cheese, and yogurt.

Healthy bones can weaken and break. Older people sometimes develop a disease called osteoporosis (say os-tee-oh-PUH-roh-sis), in which their bones are so weak that they break very easily. Sometimes the bones of osteoporosis sufferers are so weak that if they sneeze, they can break a rib.

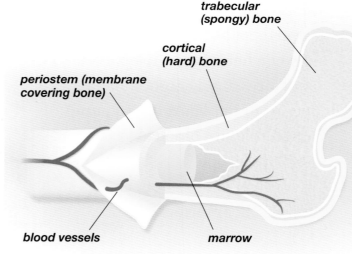

trabecular (spongy) bone

cortical (hard) bone

periostem (membrane covering bone)

blood vessels

marrow

Bones have three layers to protect the marrow in the center.

HEALTH PROFESSIONALS: Orthopedic Surgeons

Orthopedic surgeons are surgeons who specialize in operating on bones, joints, and muscles. Orthopedic surgeons mend broken bones, replace worn-out joints, and repair **tendons**.

Joints

Joints are the places where one bone meets another. Many joints move, such as those in the knees, fingers, jaw, and shoulders. Other joints do not move, such as those in the skull.

Moving joints are protected by **cartilage** and a liquid called synovial (say si-NOH-vee-uhl) fluid, which prevents the bones from rubbing together. Over time, cartilage can wear away, and joints can become swollen and sore. Some people develop a disease called arthritis, which occurs when joints rub against each other. Some people may have operations to replace their knees or hips, because these joints become so painful that they cannot move properly.

This person has a plaster cast on her arm to keep it still while the broken bone heals.

FIRST AID ✚

Treating Broken Bones
If someone has broken a bone, try to keep the person still while an ambulance is called. Moving a broken bone can cause more damage and delay healing.

GLOSSARY WORDS

blood vessels	tubes, such as veins or arteries, which blood travels through
marrow	a soft, jellylike substance in the center of bones
tendons	tough substances that connect bones to muscles
cartilage	a strong, flexible substance that cushions bones at the joints

Brain

The brain is the central processor that controls all the functions of the body. The brain, together with the spinal cord and nerves, forms the **nervous system**.

Structure of the Brain

The brain is a mass of nerve cells called neurones. It weighs about 3.3 pounds (1.5 kilograms). It is protected by the skull, a **membrane** called the meninges, and a liquid called cerebrospinal fluid.

Functions of the Brain

Different parts of the brain perform different functions.

- The brain stem controls the muscles.
- The frontal lobe controls memory, emotions, and language.
- The parietal, temporal, and occipital lobes process information from the senses, including touch, hearing, and sight.

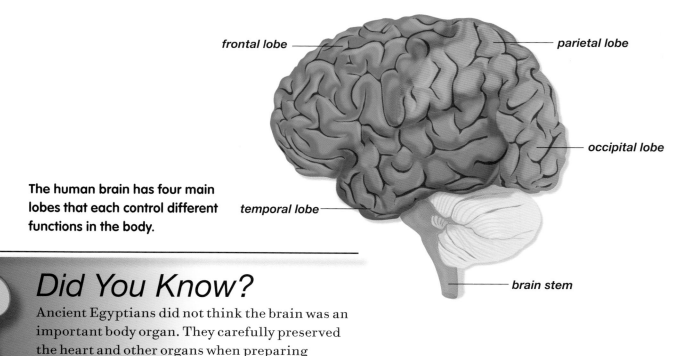

frontal lobe

parietal lobe

occipital lobe

temporal lobe

brain stem

The human brain has four main lobes that each control different functions in the body.

Did You Know?

Ancient Egyptians did not think the brain was an important body organ. They carefully preserved the heart and other organs when preparing mummies, but they discarded the brain.

Strokes

A stroke occurs when the flow of blood to part of the brain is stopped. This might be caused by a **blood clot** blocking a **blood vessel**, or by a broken blood vessel. Nearby brain cells are killed, because they do not receive enough oxygen, which travels in the blood.

The effects of a stroke vary, depending on the part of the brain in which it occurs. Some people become paralyzed or are unable to speak after a stroke. Others recover fully from strokes, but it may take months of treatment.

Concussion

If someone receives a hard hit on the head, his or her brain can bang against the skull and become bruised. This is called a concussion. A concussion is usually temporary and **symptoms** include confusion, dizziness, headaches, and even short loss of consciousness. Most people with concussions recover fully, but they do not remember what happened while they were concussed.

Baseball players avoid concussion and other head injuries by wearing helmets when batting.

HEALTH PROFESSIONALS: Neurosurgeons

Neurosurgeons are trained doctors who perform operations on the brain or spinal cord. They repair damage from head injuries and strokes, as well as remove brain tumors.

GLOSSARY WORDS

nervous system	a system of nerves, cells, and tissues that controls how the body functions
membrane	a thin layer of tissue
blood clot	a clump of semisolid blood
blood vessel	tube, such as a vein or artery, which blood travels through
symptoms	signs that a person may be suffering from a particular disease or illness

Burns

Burns can occur when skin comes into contact with very high temperatures, lightning, electricity, sunlight, or certain chemicals.

Types of Burns

Some burns are minor while others can be life-threatening. There are three types of burns.

- First-degree burns, or superficial burns, damage the top layer of skin. They appear red and feel painful.

- Second-degree burns, or partial thickness burns, damage the top two layers of skin. Skin will blister, peel, and may weep fluid. They appear red or swollen and feel extremely painful.

- Third-degree burns, or full thickness burns, damage the skin and the muscle and nerves underneath. They appear black or white as the skin has been **charred**. These are the most severe type of burns.

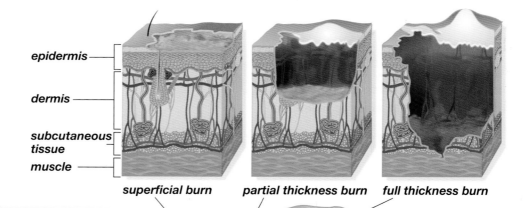

epidermis

dermis

subcutaneous tissue

muscle

superficial burn   **partial thickness burn**   **full thickness burn**

Fiona Wood (1958–)

Australian plastic surgeon Dr. Fiona Wood specializes in treating burns. She has received many awards for treating patients in emergencies, such as bomb attacks, plane crashes, and bushfires.

The skin can be damaged by first-degree, second-degree, or third-degree burns.

Skin Grafts

People with large partial thickness and full thickness burns are often given skin grafts, as the burned skin cannot heal itself. A skin graft is an operation in which burned skin is cut away and replaced with healthy skin taken from another part of the body. Australian **plastic surgeon** Dr. Fiona Wood invented spray-on skin, a process in which new skin cells are grown quickly in a **laboratory**, for use in skin grafts.

Burns in Young Children

Young children have sensitive skin and can be burned or **scalded** easily. Even hot water from a tap could cause third-degree burns in a young child. Many children suffer burns because they do not understand that some hot things can be dangerous, such as hot saucepans or heaters.

Holding burned skin under cool, running water can relieve pain.

Treating Burns

If a person is burned or scalded, hold the burn under cool, running water for up to 20 minutes. This cools the skin and relieves pain. A person with burns on a significant area of his or her body should be taken to a hospital immediately.

FIRST AID +

GLOSSARY WORDS

charred	blackened and burned by very high temperatures
plastic surgeon	a specially trained doctor who operates on skin
laboratory	a room in which scientists conduct experiments
scalded	burned by hot liquid or steam

Index

Page references in bold indicate that there is a full entry for that topic.